A 31-D/

C000155967

GIVING
BIRTH TO
HOPE

YVONNE FRANK MOORE, MD

MARIGOLD PRESS BOOKS

A division of International School of Story

Copyright © 2024 Yvonne Frank Moore
ISBN: 978-1-942923-74-9

Published in Savannah, Georgia by Marigold Press Books, a division of International School of Story.

Marigold Press Books titles may be purchased in bulk for educational, business, fund-raising, or sales promotional use. For information, please email marigoldpressbooks@gmail.com.

Fonts and stock images licensed for commercial use.

GIVING BIRTH TO

HOPE

Dedication

This book is dedicated to the memory of my maternal grandmother, Isabell Smoot McFarland Johnson aka MaDear. She was the strongest and most resourceful woman I have ever known. She was tragically widowed in 1940 when the youngest of her three girls was only eight months old. She worked long hours as a domestic and later in a mattress factory to provide for her girls. When she could have been done raising children, she "adopted" me and raised me as if I were her 4th daughter. When I was between the ages of 9 and 18 it was just the two of us. She was a praying woman of great faith who taught me by example that with God, we always have hope. Anything I have ever accomplished and all that I am I owe to MaDear. I am convinced that it was her prayers for me when I did not have enough sense to pray for myself that saved my life. Never underestimate the power of a praying grandmother!

This book of autobiographical devotionals is my way of saying, "thank you."

Contents

My Little Sanctified Self

Some of my earliest memories are about wowing adults at the age of four by reciting the books of the Bible in order. It was my grandmother's claim to fame! Whenever we had company, my grandmother would have me recite them. I quickly learned that the way to get grownups to like you was to be smart. My grandmother, who eventually raised me, had very little to do with teaching me about the Bible. Both my mother and grandmother worked full-time, so during the week, I stayed in the home of our cousin, Sister Addie Boswell.

This cousin ran an in-home preschool. She was also a devout member of the Church of God in Christ (COGIC). We went to church every time the doors were open. During the week she taught us all about God and the Bible and how to find Bible verses without using the table of contents. I am not sure how we learned to recite the books of the Bible because we could not yet read but learn them we did!

Attending church services with Sister Boswell made quite an impression on me. In the Church of God in Christ praising the Lord was very demonstrative, loud, and just plain fun. No one fell asleep during those services! My favorite aspect of worship was what I called the "Holy Dance." When I would go home on the weekends, I would demonstrate to my family how to do it, and they laughed and made fun of my little sanctified self. As I grew older, I witnessed multiple adult family members who were saints on Sunday but broke all of the Ten Commandments the rest of the week! Looking back on it now, I realize that I lived in two different worlds, one spiritual and one secular. Is it any wonder that I grew up confused about the things of God?

Children are very impressionable, and they learn about life and truth from watching the adults around them. Ask yourself if the life you are living matches up with what you say you believe. If you want to not only be blessed but be a blessing to those around you, do everything in your power to live an upright and godly life.

"But let him ask in faith, with no doubting, for the one who doubts is like a wave of the sea that is driven and tossed by the wind. For that person must not suppose that he will receive anything from the Lord; he is a double-minded man, unstable in all his ways." James 1:6-8 ESV

PRAYER

Heavenly Father, please make us mindful of the influence we have on the children in our lives. Help us to live lives that honor You and that are consistent with what we teach our children.

Waiting for My Daddy

I know that I was not the only little girl who adored her daddy. I am also sure that I was not the only little girl to be hurt by that same daddy. My parents split when I was only two years old, so I have no memory of actually living with him. But I do remember always being excited to see him!

I can vividly remember so many times sitting on the top step of my grandmother's porch with my little clothes in a brown paper grocery bag waiting for my daddy to pick me up for the weekend. More often than not, he would fail to show up. You see, my father was a weekend drunk who would make promises during the week that alcohol kept him from keeping on the weekends.

I can recall a stretch of time when I did not see him for nearly two years even though we lived in the same city. I came to the conclusion that the reason he never had a phone was because he did not want me to have a way to get in touch with him.

Thanks to my grandmother, who raised me, and a mother who visited us twice a year, as well as the summers I spent in Maryland with my mom and my stepfather, I had a pretty stable upbringing. However, I never stopped wanting to have a relationship with my daddy.

Once I became an adult, I made it my mission to have him in my life. He still lived in the same broken-down duplex he had always lived in, still did not have a phone and he was still drinking heavily. I had a phone installed and helped him pay his bills. He was content to continue to live the way he did, so I had to respect that. At least now I could check on him from time to time.

I was raised to believe the Ten Commandments dictate that we honor our parents regardless of whether they were good parents or not. My mother and her family made sure I knew that my dad never contributed to the expenses of my upbringing. He was the original deadbeat dad! In spite of that, I still held on to the fantasy of being "daddy's little girl."

Fast forward 20 years when my daddy fell into ill health. By then I had married and was going through a divorce and had two kids of my own. The last thing I wanted to do was to take care of someone who had little or no contact with me when I needed him. For the first time I can remember, I got down on my face and cried out to God to take the bitterness from my heart and help me see my daddy the way I did before all the disappointments. It was miraculous how God answered that prayer.

The very next day when I went to see my dad in the hospital, my heart overflowed with a childlike love, and all I wanted to do was to care for him and let him know how much I loved him. For the rest of his life, that is exactly what I did, taking him to all of his doctor's appointments, making sure he ate, and even moving him in with my kids and me for a short time when it was no longer safe for him to be alone.

If there is someone in your life you simply cannot forgive, take it to God. By the power of His Holy Spirit, He will gently wipe away the bitterness and replace it with the grace and mercy He shows to us all. If He did it for me, He can do it for you too!

"Instead, be kind to each other, tenderhearted, forgiving one another, just as God through Christ has forgiven you." Ephesians 4:32 NLT

PRAYER

Dear Lord, thank You for the love that You put inside each of us for our parents. Honoring them is so important to You that You commanded us to do it in Your Word. Please do not allow circumstances beyond our control keep us from loving those You have instructed us to love.

Shoebox Fried Chicken

When I was a small child, once a year my grandmother and I would go by train to visit her brother, "Uncle Sam," in Chicago. We were just like hundreds of other black families who had participated in the northward migration and now had relatives who lived "up north."

Like many of my childhood memories, my recollections of these trips revolve around food. Before every trip my grandmother would fry up some chicken and place it in a wax paper lined shoebox. I can still conjure up the smell of my grandmother's delicious fried chicken that was released when she opened the shoebox on the train.

Eating that chicken out of the shoebox was always the highlight of the trips for me, along with the fresh chocolate chip cookies my great uncle bought for me at the train station in Chicago! (Did I mention how much I loved to eat as a child???)

What I experienced as one of the pure joys of my childhood has become tainted by my later learning that we took food with us on our train trips to Chicago because that was the only way for us to have food on those long journeys. How was I to know there were dining cars on those very same trains? I did not know about them because dining cars back then were subject to the segregation rules of the states where they traveled. I do not remember it being discussed, it was just a fact of life in the south in the 1950's.

I have come to understand that what we refer to today as "white privilege" has its roots in the way whites and blacks had separate everything, and the Colored version was always inferior to what white people had. We even got the raggedy cast-off books from the white schools already marked up and sometimes with pages missing.

My elementary school was segregated so I did not go to school with white kids until seventh grade. I do not remember what the percentages were, but we were definitely in the minority! Being separate was such a way of life for us that we self-segregated in the cafeteria and at pep rallies. It took a while for us to feel comfortable with mixed socializing, not because of dislike so much as distrust.

To this day, I see self-segregation play out in our churches, book clubs and social organizations. Wanting to spend time with others who look and act and talk and think like us is, I believe, instinctual. Even though that may be true, we will never truly get past the invisible walls that divide us until we share our lives and cultures in meaningful ways that will help us to understand why all of us think the way we do. When it is all said and done, the true path to racial harmony begins in our hearts and our minds.

"For as he thinks in his heart, so is he."
Proverbs 23:7 NKJV

PRAYER

Dear Lord, help us to see each other as You see us. Each of us is made in Your image so that none of us can boast that we are any better than the other. Please keep us ever mindful that we are all Your precious daughters and sons.

Grandma Sally's Satchel

After my mother's death from a second massive stroke in 2019, I had the grim task of planning her funeral. I was her only child, and she had lost her husband several years before. As I was going through her effects, looking for pictures and important papers, I came across her birth certificate. There it was on an aged official document - proof that my mother had been delivered by her own paternal great grandmother, Sally McFarland! I had heard stories all my life from my maternal grandmother that her husband's grandmother had delivered my mother and both her sisters at home in the 1930's.

My grandmother had never been told anything about labor even after she was pregnant. She actually thought that the brown line down the middle of her tummy would just pop open so the baby could get out. Grandma Sally, as she was called by everyone, was one of many "Granny" midwives who delivered babies in the segregated South. She assisted the deliveries of both black and white women in the rural town of Edmondson, Arkansas. Her skill for delivering babies had been passed down to her from our ancestors who brought their skills from Africa and practiced them during slavery.

Slave midwives were valued by plantation owners because they helped to ensure that slave babies were born healthy in order to perpetuate slave labor. During Grandma Sally's lifetime, her skills were valued in the black community because there were no black doctors in her small southern town, and laws of segregation prohibited hospitalization in the white-only hospital.

My mother and her siblings loved telling the story of Grandma Sally's satchel. According to them, Grandma Sally always carried a large satchel whenever she went to someone's house to deliver a baby. My mom and her two male cousins were playmates, and they were all forbidden to ever touch Grandma Sally's satchel. They never saw what was inside. All they knew was that when Grandma Sally went to someone's house with that satchel, there was a brand-new baby when she left. So, what else were they supposed to think as little kids but that Grandma Sally carried babies in that Satchel? It was not until they were older that they realized that in her Satchel she carried the tools needed to deliver babies.

My great-great-grandmother, Sally, did not pass her midwifery skills down to her immediate descendants, but our family continued to take pride in her role as a midwife long after her death.

I went into medical school with the notion that I would become a gynecologist, because I wanted to teach women about their bodies and how to care for them. I had taken a Women's Studies course in college that convinced me that my fellow students, as smart as they were, knew very little about their bodies (not unlike my grandmother all those years ago). It was not until I did my obstetrics rotation as a 3rd year medical student that I quickly realized there was nothing in medicine as exciting as seeing a new life come into the world! I was hooked at my very first delivery!

I went on to become an obstetrician/gynecologist and to deliver many hundreds of babies over the next 35 years. I have often wondered if my love for obstetrics was born out of years of hearing stories about Grandma Sally. In the same way that musical talent appears to run in some families, could it be that God led me to obstetrics because He knew that the passion and talent for delivering babies was in my genes? After all, the blood of Grandma Sally runs through my veins. I will never cease to be amazed at how God weaves whatever he has placed inside of us to achieve His purpose for our lives.

"For it is God who works in you to will and to act in order to fulfill his good purpose." Philippians 2:13 NIV

PRAYER

Lord, we thank You for all of the gifts and talents You have placed inside each of us. Help us to embrace those gifts and use them for Your glory!

MaDear My Adoptive Mother

Mother's Day is always bittersweet to me. As happy as I am to be celebrated by my children, my heart still aches with missing the lady who raised me and molded me into the woman I have become. Not a day goes by when I don't hear her voice coming from my mouth. I feel as if her spirit is within me.

My grandmother, Isabell Smoot McFarland Johnson (aka MaDear), was strong, opinionated, feisty and absolutely one of a kind. I praise God for the wonderful memories I have of my MaDear. One of the reasons this book came to be is that she was fond of saying that she could write a book about this or that subject. As I spoke at her funeral, I recalled hearing that from her so many times, and I decided that someone in our family needed to write the book she never got to write. I promised I would get it done!

I often wonder what would have become of me if my grandmother had not been willing to raise me. It was not uncommon in the black community in the 50's and prior for women to leave their children "Down South" to be raised by their own parents while they moved north for better job opportunities.

Prior to my mother moving to the D.C. area, my grandmother and I lived on one side of a duplex while my mother and her abusive boyfriend lived on the other. Whenever I would go to my mother asking for permission to do something or go someplace, her response was invariably, "Go ask MaDear."

My grandmother was definitely in charge of me. I was more like her youngest daughter than her grandchild. When my mom would go out partying and not return until the next day, I listened to MaDear fussing about how no one who had a child should be out all night. I was that pesky "baby sister" who enjoyed seeing my mom get in trouble with her mom.

When my mother decided to move to the D.C. area with my aunt and her husband to escape the boyfriend whose beatings had once landed her in the hospital, she did not take me. I was told that if we both left, MaDear would be all alone and none of us wanted that. The way I saw it in my nine-year old brain, it was my responsibility to look after my grandmother. Never mind that my grandmother was a strong, vibrant, 51-year old woman who worked full time, was a leader in the union at the factory where she worked and was still dating, I agreed that "she needed me."

The truth is that I had no memory of ever NOT living with my grandmother, so I did not want to move to D.C. I could not imagine life without her! As time went on, I began to think of myself as being adopted by my grandmother. She gave me what every child needs - a sense of belonging. Anything that I have accomplished in this life I owe to her steady guidance and her prayers. Hers was the earthly example of what God has given us when He adopts us into His family and gives us the privilege of being called His children.

There is no bigger blessing than that.

"He predestined us for adoption to himself as sons through Jesus Christ, according to the purpose of his will . . ." Ephesians 1:5 ESV

PRAYER

Heavenly Father, thank You for all those who adopt children as an extension of their love for You and adoption by You into Your family. You have shown us by Your unconditional love the example of what it means to lovingly parent adopted children. We thank You for the sacrifices they make.

Hope After Abuse

During my teen years, I spent summers with my mother and future stepfather in D.C. My mother lived in a second floor, stairwell entrance apartment with my aunt and her husband. By the time I was 14, I was very overweight and had to wear clothes in women's sizes. My aunt's husband was in the military but came home from his nearby base on the weekends. He was a perfectly nice guy and a good uncle, always teaching me and encouraging me to be a good student. Except when he was drunk.

There is a day burned into my brain: I was wearing a yellow checkered dress, and my uncle and I were alone in the apartment. He sidled up to me and offered me $20 to let him kiss me! When I screamed "NO!" he kept coming toward me. I knew he was drunk, but I also knew he was stronger than me. I was terrified that he would overpower me and do God-knows-what to me. I had the good sense to make it into a bedroom, slam the door and push the chest of drawers in front of the door so he couldn't get in.

I was still very upset when my mother got home. When I told her what happened, she blew me off by saying that he was "just drunk." Then she made me promise not to tell my grandmother, because she would never let me come back to D.C. the next summer!

So many women have stories just like mine - only they were not lucky enough to get away! It was a dirty little secret back then that sexual abuse at the hands of a family member was so common that it was often ignored.

I have read the accounts of so many women who carried the scars of such encounters secretly into adulthood. When our own parents won't stand up for us, we start thinking we don't matter. The good news is that no matter how unworthy we have been made to feel, God's love never changes.

If you are harboring shame and low self-esteem because of what someone did to you in childhood, please know that you are still valuable in the eyes of God. Consider seeking counseling from a Christian mental health provider who can help you to develop coping skills to deal with the trauma of your past.

"Yet I will certainly bring health and healing to it and will indeed heal them. I will let them experience the abundance of true peace." Jeremiah 33:6 CSB

PRAYER

Heavenly Father, you know every instance of abuse that each of us has suffered as children. Help us learn to forgive those who have mistreated us. Please do not allow those bad memories to make us forget that You love us unconditionally and that You always will.

Sin Sampler
Hope for Prodigals

God has blessed me to have more than a few experiences over the course of my life that have equipped me to be that older woman to whom younger women turn for advice. I have been blessed with so many young women in my practice and in my life who are going where I have already been. It is my fervent prayer that I have learned from my experiences how to live a godly life and that I might be able to pass along some of what I have learned to younger women.

When I was that younger woman myself, particularly in my teens and twenties, I did not seek the counsel of godly older women and found myself knee deep in all sorts of sin. When I look back on my college and medical school days, I marvel that I survived. Because I was raised by a very strict grandmother,

her rules kept me from participating in many of the activities my peers were allowed to do in high school. Going away to college gave me the freedom to make my own decisions, and I made some really bad ones! You name it, I did it! From indiscriminate sex to binge drinking and many things in between - it was as if I wanted to sample everything on the sin menu!

The very first weekend I was away at school I went to a house party in a rough part of town with a girl I had just met. I found myself in the backseat of a car with a couple of her male friends, smoking marijuana and letting them give me "shotguns." You would think that someone who was salutatorian of her high school class would have better sense. I had never even smelled marijuana until that very night. Thank God there was no social media back then to record all my foolishness!

Later during my freshman year, I was dumped by my high school boyfriend because my studies left no time for me to be with him. This was the church boy my grandmother had hand-picked for me. (She had no idea that I had lost my virginity to him on her living room couch.) When he wanted to propose marriage to me over Christmas break, she went with him to pick out my engagement ring!

When he broke up with me, I was relieved that I would no longer have the pressure of trying to maintain a relationship and keep my grades up. I rationalized that the solution for me would be to take up with a much older married man (who was separated but not divorced) who would be less demanding of my time, because he had a family to think about. This guy and three of his married buddies rented a house where they could bring their side chicks to party. I cringe now when I think of how someone raised in church could have had such low moral standards.

I relate tales from my days spent trying the sin sampler not to brag but to make the point that no one is so far gone that God cannot bring you back into the fold and use you for His purposes. You know you were not raised to be doing everything the opposite of what you were taught, but you are out there doing it anyway because you too have fallen for the devil's lies.

Let me tell you, you can make a u-turn this very day and return to your First Love. He is waiting for you with open arms. That is what grace and mercy is all about! The very moment you repent of your sin and stop doing whatever it is, you get a clean slate as if it never happened. I know that sounds too good to be true, but I have lived it and I know it to be true.

"'I have told you my commands. But you do not listen to me any longer. You have not obeyed me, even since the time of your ancestors. Now, return to me! Then I will return to bless you.' That is what the Lord Almighty says. But you ask, 'How do we return to you?'" Malachi 3:7 EAS

PRAYER

Father God, I pray right now for every prodigal daughter and son out there who has strayed away from the faith in which they were raised. I pray that they will repent and return to their relationship with You. Let them know that the blood of Jesus has already guaranteed their forgiveness. They do not have to wait to "get right." We are thankful that You will take us just as we are.

Ambitions Don't Die They Evolve

I am often asked how a little, black girl born into poverty in the segregated fifties grew up to become a doctor. It is funny how the ambitions of a child change over time. Growing up, there was a family up the street who had a set of twins I idolized. They were a year older than me and went to a nearby Catholic school, so I wanted to go there as well. On the first day of school, my mother took me to that school all dressed in the school uniform of a navy skirt and white blouse, only to be told that registration had been closed weeks before and it was too late for me to register.

To this day, I still remember how heartbroken I was! My mother took me down the street to the public school. I was still crying when she took me to join Mrs. Young's class. Mrs. Young consoled me and hugged me and assured me that everything was going to be alright. From that day and for the rest of the year, I was the teacher's pet. My love for Mrs. Young made me certain that I would be a teacher when I grew up.

That is, until my eighth grade English teacher recommended me for our junior high newspaper staff. I was already a budding news junkie, watching the CBS evening news with Walter Cronkite every weekday after school, so I was very excited to work on our little newspaper. Encouraged by the accolades I received from teachers for the articles and especially the editorials I wrote, I became convinced that I would pursue a career as a writer.

That is, until 10th grade when I was NOT chosen to be a member of my high school newspaper staff. My aspirations to become a journalist/writer ended (or so I thought) right then and there.

As a big fan of the Perry Mason TV series, I joined my high school debate team, because I thought I would learn what it would be like to be a lawyer arguing cases. I learned a lot about myself as a member of the debate team. I enjoyed the research and worked hard at it. I did not, however, like arguing a point I did not believe in.

When you are near the top of your class in high school, others expect you to go on to college and beyond, even if no one else in your family has ever been to college. Church members were telling me that I should go to either law school or medical school.

My experience as a member of the debate team had shown me that law school was out and I had never met or heard of a doctor who looked like me, so I internally dismissed pursuing those professions. Prior to college I did spend a summer doing volunteer work in a D.C. area hospital, and I was very drawn to the idea of working in a hospital helping others. I was surprised how comfortable I felt at the hospital, like I belonged there.

By then I had also developed a passion for sports, not as a participant but as a fan. I was in awe of the way athletes trained and pushed their bodies to achieve their goals. While my friends had pictures of the Jackson Five on their walls, I had one of my favorite baseball players, legendary pitcher, Bob Gibson, on my wall.

My stepfather, who was one of the smartest people I had ever met, suggested I should become a physical therapist. Pursuing a degree in physical therapy would not take nearly as long as medical school and would allow me to work with athletes. So when I went to Washington University as a biology/psychology double major, it was with the intent of becoming a physical therapist! My dream job in 1972 was to ultimately become a trainer to an NBA team and travel the country to games.

That is, until my biology advisor at Washington University informed me that I was already taking the same classes to get into physical therapy school that I would take to get into medical school and doing quite well. Until that day in his office, the thought of being a doctor had never been a serious consideration. In fact, I was so sure I couldn't do it that I became a "closet premed." No one except my advisor knew that I was going to try to get into medical school! It wasn't until I was accepted at both Washington University and St. Louis University medical schools that I announced to family and friends that I was going to study to become a doctor! The rest, as they say, is history.

The reflections that have been required to write this book have made me realize that all of my childhood aspirations have been fulfilled in one way or another. As an ObGyn physician, I see myself as a teacher as I explain to my patients how their bodies work and how they can improve their health. My fascination with athletes and love of travel morphed into my becoming a distance interval runner at age 59, achieving a goal of completing a half marathon in every state. My dreams of someday being a writer have come to fruition both as a blogger and in crafting the book you hold in your hand.

Pastor Tony Evans is quoted as saying, "If all you know is what you see, then you will never see all that is to be seen." My finite mind would never allow me to dream of something I had never seen - a black female physician. But God's dreams and plans for you are beyond anything you could ever imagine. If my life is a testimony to anything to children growing up today, it is that God wants us to dream big! Just because you have never seen something does not mean it cannot be done!

"However, as it is written: 'No eye has seen, no ear has heard, and no human mind has conceived the things God has prepared for those who love him.'" 1 Corinthians 2:9 NIV

PRAYER

Father God, You are the giver of dreams and the Master of our lives. Lead us and guide so that we may make the decisions that line up with Your will for us. Reassure us that we do not have to understand every assignment, we just have to trust You.

The Enduring Weight of Childhood Obesity

I have struggled with my weight my entire life. I was raised by a single grandmother who was a great cook. Weekend breakfasts often included homemade biscuits with ham and red eye gravy and rice. That has to be at least a zillion carbs! I was a bookworm from an early age, so the only exercise I got was in gym class. One of the more painful memories of my childhood was of having to order special gym clothes because I was too big for the standard sizes.

Back then, we did not have the obesity epidemic we have today, so plus-sized children were far less common. I can remember being teased and bullied about my weight, which I countered with self-deprecating humor. I told the toughest girl in junior high that she didn't scare me because I didn't have to fight her, all I had to do was sit on her! We eventually became friends. I compensated for not being able to do what others could do athletically by being the best possible student I could be and by making good grades.

By the time I was 14, I tipped the scales at 185 lbs and wore a women's size 18-20! By then my mother had moved to the D.C. area to escape an abusive relationship and met the man who was soon to become my stepfather. I rarely saw my biological father and really wanted my mother to get married to someone nice. They told me that if I lost 20 lbs, they would get married. They may have been teasing me, but I took the notion seriously. That was the moment when I went on the first of many diets.

That diet was self-made and simple: no breakfast, a green salad and a diet soda for lunch and a single serving of whatever we had for dinner (as opposed to the seconds and thirds I usually had). I don't remember how long it took but I lost that 20 pounds and got myself a new stepfather in the bargain! I was down to a junior size 15, and my grandmother no longer had to struggle to find age-appropriate clothes for me.

People in my life who have only known me as an adult think that I have always been the size that I am now. Few know of the many, many diets I have been on over the course of my life, all because I was terrified that I would balloon back up to the miserable, obese girl I was at 15. Even as a normal sized adult, that overweight teenager and the pain she endured have fueled my efforts to be the healthiest me I can be and to help others do the same.

What scars are you carrying from your childhood? Have they left you with feelings of unworthiness that have followed you into adulthood? That kind of thinking is a trick the enemy uses to keep you from living up to your potential.

When one of those thoughts of inferiority enters your head, take that thought captive and replace it with the truth found in God's word. Learn to see yourself the way our loving God sees you. When He looks at you, He sees you as His child that was made in his own image. We are all fearfully and wonderfully made and worthy to be loved.

"For you formed my inward parts; you knitted me in my mother's womb. I praise you, for I am fearfully and wonderfully made. Wonderful are your works; my soul knows it very well." Psalm 139:13-14 ESV

PRAYER

Dear Lord, we thank You that You have made each of us unique and that You do not make mistakes. Please do not let others make us forget that no matter what we see in the mirror, we are made in Your image and are worthy of love.

What God Has for You is For You

It plays in my mind like a scene in a movie. There I stood, in front of a list of the people who had been chosen for the Central High School newspaper staff, looking for my name. I must have looked at the list too fast! I looked a second time, this time more slowly, line by line. Much to my disbelief, my name was not there! How could that be?

I was an excellent student and I had come to think of being smart as my "superpower." I had been one of the more prolific writers on my junior high newspaper and had been encouraged by my teachers to believe that I was a good writer. In fact, I had fallen in love with writing as a member of that newspaper staff and had aspirations to become a professional journalist. How could that ever be possible if I was not even good enough to make my high school paper? I was crushed.

Never to be one to question the authority of my teachers, I accepted the decision and joined the yearbook staff instead. In the many years that have passed since that day, I have often wondered why I was excluded.

My high school had only become integrated a few years before my arrival, and when I started in 1969 it still had a very low percentage of black students. As a ninth grader I had written editorials for my junior high newspaper about the importance of the civil rights movement and black pride.

A small group of us participated in one of the marches on behalf of striking sanitation workers in Memphis where we were tear gassed just for being there. The James Brown song, "Say it Loud, I'm Black and I'm proud," provided the inspiration for one of the editorials I wrote for the paper shortly after that. Only much later did I learn that my activities and writings in junior high played a role in making me an unsuitable candidate for the high school newspaper staff.

Was I a victim of racism or was there something much more consequential at work? Even though not making the newspaper staff was a huge disappointment, it forced me to open my mind to other career possibilities.

I had no idea at the time that it would be my destiny to become a physician and deliver hundreds of babies! I had no idea that God would use me the way He has to minister both physically and spiritually to so many of His precious people.

God knows the plans He has for each one of us. If the direction you are going in does not line up with those plans, He will provide a course correction that may seem like a disappointment in real time but eventually will fit into the tapestry of your life. All He asks you to do is trust Him!

"For we are God's handiwork, created in Christ Jesus to do good works, which God prepared in advance for us to do." Ephesians 2:10 NIV

PRAYER

Dear God, sometimes we do not understand what You are doing in our lives when what we think we want does not line up with Your ultimate plan for our lives. Help us to recognize Your sovereignty and trust You no matter what.

It's Never Too Late
My Running Journey

I have loved sports for as long as I can remember. I loved to WATCH sports, but participation was another thing entirely. Because I was a chubby little girl and adolescent, I struggled with doing anything physical. I could never jump rope, was terrible at hopscotch and did not learn to ride a bike until I was nearly 13 years old. In gym class we had to do long jumps, high jumps and run laps in order to pass physical fitness tests, and I wasn't good at any of those activities. When we played basketball in class, I was always the last one chosen. Needless to say, I came to hate gym class.

Perhaps it was because I felt so completely inept at anything physical, I was in awe of professional athletes and their abilities. When my friends were all abuzz about the Jackson 5, I had a major crush on pitcher Bob Gibson and I had become a die-hard fan of the St. Louis Cardinals. When the Cardinals played on the west coast, I would have my transistor radio under my pillow listening to the games late into the night! It wasn't just baseball, I watched professional football and basketball as well. During the Olympics I was glued to the television, especially for the track and field events. My inner athlete lived vicariously through my heroes in the world of sports.

By the time I went away to college in St Louis, I had lost some of the weight and decided to take a tennis class for my physical education requirement. I would like to tell you that I found my niche on the tennis court, but alas, that too was a miserable failure.

In my 30's I discovered exercise videos and enjoyed using those because no one else was watching to see whether I could keep up. Those videos were my main form of physical activity for most of my adult life. I still enjoy them to this day and have found an endless variety of workout videos on YouTube to incorporate into my daily exercise routine.

At some point in my late 50's one of my patients invited me to join a fitness group that ran and walked on Saturday mornings. I had never considered becoming a runner, but I had started doing neighborhood walks in addition to my exercise videos so I thought I would be able to keep up with the walkers in the group.

During my first session, I tried to keep up with the fast walkers and had to trot a little just to keep up with them. Even though I was huffing and puffing, I really enjoyed the brisk walking mixed with a little jogging that enabled me to keep up. As members of the group we agreed to participate in local 5K races. Even though I was slow by "real runner" standards, I found great satisfaction in the excitement of the races, the cheering spectators and the sense of accomplishment I felt every time I crossed a finish line.

After doing numerous local 5Ks and 10Ks, I was encouraged by the other ladies to train to do the half marathon the group planned to travel to do in Puerto Rico. To convince myself that I could actually finish a half marathon, I signed up for and completed my very first half marathon in my home town at the age of 59. I found the 13.1 mile distance to be quite challenging, but it left me with the desire to do it again. Over the next 10 years I completed that distance in every state, D.C., Puerto Rico, Canada and Mexico!

Throughout my journey, I have continued to use the strategy of interval running where I walk briskly between intervals of jogging (which I call wogging). At this writing I have completed 85 official half marathons as an interval runner. That non-athletic chubby little girl has morphed into a distance runner in her 60's!

Look at God!!!

I give God all the glory for knowing I had this ability inside me all along; I only lacked the courage to tap into it. The highlight of my year every year for the last 10 years is running the St. Jude half marathon as a hero, raising funds for St Jude's Children's Research Hospital. Running through the hospital campus to the cheers of those precious children and their families gives purpose to my running. I consider any other race I do as training to run on behalf of the kids. Nothing that has happened to me in my life has surprised or gratified me more than my life as a runner!

If there is a take home from my journey from non athletic little girl to distance interval runner it is that our God is a God of possibilities. I now believe that in spite of how I saw myself, God saw something different! Part of His unexpected plan for my life was be an example, proving that with God's help it is never too late to do things that you might never have imagined for yourself. Walking and running have improved both my physical and mental health as I enter the eighth decade of life. When I tell my patients that "movement is medicine," I now have a testimony to back it up. I like to think that I am the poster girl for active aging!

"Jesus looked at them intently and said, 'Humanly speaking, it is impossible. But with God everything is possible.'" Matthew 19:26 NLT

PRAYER

Father God, we thank You for the big dreams that You put on our hearts that we would never dream in our finite minds. Thank You for the strength You give us to do that which pleases You and accomplishes Your purpose for our lives.

Abortion Provider Sees the Truth

Recently, our Sunday School lesson was about the transformation of Saul, who went from persecuting the followers of Jesus, to "Paul," who Jesus himself assigned to carry the good news to those who did not yet believe in Him. Paul's story of redemption and grace resonates with me on a personal level.

After I graduated from medical school, I returned to Memphis for a residency in ObGyn at the University of Tennessee. It was well-known within our residency program that the most lucrative and sought after moonlighting jobs were found in the three local abortion clinics. I knew there were good residents who chose not to do abortions for religious reasons, but I never really understood what one thing had to do with the other. My best friend in college had an abortion, and I had been very supportive of her decision at the time. We were thankful that the Supreme Court had made abortion legal the year after we started college.

It seemed only logical that when I was offered the chance to provide those services, I had an obligation to do it. After all, if doctors who believed in a woman's right to choose didn't do abortions, who else would? By the time I was a senior resident, I was the medical director of one of the local abortion clinics and spent my vacation time at pro-abortion seminars and political functions. I was proud that I was doing my part to protect a woman's right to choose and to have autonomy over her own body.

It was not until I was pregnant myself that I began to really examine my feelings about the moral aspects of abortion. It had taken over a year for me to become pregnant with my daughter. The first time I saw the tiny little flicker of her heartbeat on an ultrasound screen, I fell completely in love with her. I finally had to come to terms with the fact that the only thing that made my daughter any different than all those tiny babies I had terminated was the fact that I wanted her.

Back then, after each procedure, especially those after 12 weeks, we routinely examined the contents of the collection bag. I would look at tiny arms, legs, rib cages and skulls as if it was a baby puzzle, making sure that all parts were accounted for. It was as if I had been so blinded by my commitment to a woman's right to choose that I could not see the babies represented in those perfectly formed body parts.

Once I saw my daughter, whom I had met during that first trimester sonogram, develop into my much-loved first-born child, I was at last able to see what I had not allowed myself to see in all those years of doing terminations. An abortion ends a human life. This is not a political statement; it is simply the truth that the Lord allowed me to finally see.

After my own Paul-like conversion, I went from being a politically active abortion provider to being even more active in the pro-life movement. I was keynote speaker at several pro-life fundraisers and served on the board of directors of a crisis pregnancy center; I taught classes to center volunteers on the potential complications of abortions.

My experience offered a unique perspective because I knew first hand that what is inside a pregnant woman's uterus is not simply a blob of tissue but a tiny human being whose life ends when an abortion is performed. I cannot tell you how many women have changed their minds about terminating a pregnancy once they saw their babies during a sonogram the same way I did.

I often wonder why God allowed the development of technology that lets us have a view into the womb. Just like Paul, I consider myself to once have been the "chiefest among sinners" before my conversion experience. After taking the lives of so many babies, God has not only granted me grace, mercy, and forgiveness but he has used me to share this testimony with many people and to save the lives of many unborn babies in the process. I am not proud of my history as an abortion provider, but I am humbled by the way God has used that experience for good. It is true that God's grace is real and immeasurable. If you think you have strayed too far away from God for Him to use you - think again.

"For I am convinced that neither death nor life, neither angels nor demons, neither the present nor the future, nor any powers, neither height nor depth, nor anything else in all creation, will be able to separate us from the love of God that is in Christ Jesus our Lord." Romans 8:38-39 NIV

PRAYER

Dear Lord, Thank You for the reassurance You have given us in Scripture that You love us unconditionally no matter what we do. We are grateful for the limitless grace and mercy toward us. Help us to forgive ourselves when we stumble and to see ourselves as You see us. We are thankful that You can bring good out of any situation.

Saline Solution
Medicine as Ministry

Not long ago I had the unpleasant task of telling a long-term patient that her biopsy came back indicating that she had cancer of the uterus. After her first visit with the oncologist I recommended, she called wanting to know if the doctor was a Christian. I had to answer honestly that I did not know. She had mentioned the power of prayer to the doctor, who appeared to be taken aback by the suggestion. I explained to the patient, who had become accustomed to my praying with her, that not every doctor feels comfortable sharing their faith with their patients or praying with them. I know this to be true because I used to be one of those doctors.

That conversation led to me pondering when and why I became a Christian who happens to be a doctor instead of a doctor who happens to be a

Christian - there is a difference. The answer involves a weekend over 25 years ago when I attended a conference sponsored by the Christian Medical Associations called the Saline Solution. There I was challenged to stop having two faces, a "church face" and a totally different "professional face." In doing so, I was missing the opportunity to attend to the spiritual needs of my patients. Worse, I had been brainwashed during my training into thinking that witnessing to patients is somehow unethical.

However, study after study has shown that attending religious services regularly is associated with better health outcomes and longevity. Armed with that information, I now see being open about what God has done in my life and praying with patients means bringing to bear all of what might help them heal.

Once I began to see my practice as ministry, it became so much more fulfilling. After every delivery, I would get the family to hold hands and say a short prayer of thanksgiving for the miracle of new life. Before every surgery, I would pray with the patient for guidance and a favorable outcome. In the office when someone breaks down in tears over a troubled marriage or wayward children, instead of a prescription for medication I encourage them through scripture and prayer. It is not just doctors who can see their workplace as a ministry, because all believers have been challenged in scripture to share the goodness of God in our circles of influence.

"I pray that the sharing of your faith may become effective and powerful because of your accurate knowledge of every good thing which is ours in Christ." Philemon 1:6 AMP

PRAYER

Lord, thank You for showing me how to be salt and light in places where it might be needed even if not expected. Help me to show by example that sharing our faith means bringing the best of who we are to any situation.

Pregnancy Loss
A Private Grief

In nearly 40 years as an ObGyn physician, I have had many patients who have experienced loss at various stages of pregnancy. However, I do not think I truly understood what they were going through until I had a miscarriage myself. I learned that such a loss impacts a woman in ways that her spouse/partner and other family members might not understand. Make no mistake about it, for the woman who is desperately wanting a baby, she sees not just a positive pregnancy test but she imagines an actual baby. The further along a woman is in pregnancy, the more real that baby becomes.

Even though my miscarriage was in the first trimester and was over 30 years ago, I still remember how emotionally painful it was. In my darkest moments, I turned to Scripture passages, especially

Psalm 91 to reassure me that God was still with me in the midst of my grief.

Because I had carried my first pregnancy to term, it never once occurred to me that I might miscarry. The truth is that one in every five pregnancies ends in miscarriage. When it happens early in pregnancy, no one outside your circle might even be aware you were pregnant. The overwhelming sense of loss, for me, started with questioning what I might have done wrong to cause the miscarriage. It is a question that almost every woman who experiences pregnancy loss asks herself.

No matter what I say to reassure a grieving mom that a pregnancy loss is the will of a sovereign God, there is always a sense of failure and shame that remains. This can be compounded by the fact that the spouse or partner may not be supportive or may not understand the level of grief she is going through. The loss may be an entirely different experience for him, causing him to "get over it" a lot sooner.

Unfortunately, I also have several patients who have carried their babies to term and the pregnancy ended in stillbirth or in death in the first few minutes of life. Most of the time this happens unexpectedly in what seemed to be a perfectly normal pregnancy. The mom might have been in a routine prenatal visit when we were unable to find a heartbeat. The statement, "Your baby no longer has a heartbeat" is something no mother ever wants to hear! It is her worst nightmare. Then comes the realization that she will have to endure labor and deliver that child. Each time I have witnessed such a delivery, I am convinced that God gives women an extra measure of strength to get through it.

In some cases there were fetal anomalies incompatible with life that were diagnosed during pregnancy but the mother chose to carry that child rather than terminate the pregnancy. I have so much admiration for those women and the courage it takes to carry a baby who is "born to die." In each of those cases, the women got to hold their babies and show them love, however brief the time. I have attended memorial services for some of those babies and been truly blessed by the outpouring of love and support of family and friends. The truth is that every life, no matter how brief, matters to their families and matters to God.

"Whoever dwells in the shelter of the Most High will rest in the shadow of the Almighty. I will say of the Lord, 'He is my refuge and my fortress, my God, in whom I trust.'" Psalms 91:1-2 NIV

PRAYER

Lord, we thank You for being our shelter in the storms of life. Teach us to trust You even when our prayers are not answered in the way we might have hoped. Thank You for always being there whenever we need You.

Divorce
Loss of a Dream

One of my favorite TV shows growing up was *Father Knows Best*, starring Robert Young. As my mother's only child who was raised by my grandmother, I longed for the kind of family portrayed by the Andersons - a hard working dad, a stay-at-home mom and three kids.

If the Andersons were the dream family of my childhood, as an adult, the Huxtables of the Bill Cosby Show quickly replaced them and became my updated ideal family. Cliff and Claire Huxtable were African American like me and were raising a family while also managing careers as a doctor and a lawyer, respectively. As a professional woman with a husband who was also a professional, and as parents of two children, we were well on our way to becoming real life Huxtables!

When my marriage began to unravel after 15 years, I was devastated. By then I had an active prayer life and was closer to God than I had ever been. I begged God to save my marriage and allow my children to grow up in a home with a mother AND a father - something I never had but always so desperately wanted. My fairytale, want-to-be Huxtable life came to an end despite all my prayers.

By the grace of God, I was given another chance to have a storybook romance and nearly 18 years of a godly marriage. It has now been over three years since that husband went to be with the Lord after his four-year battle with cancer. During this widowhood season of my life, I recognize I am among a subset of widows who have also experienced divorce. Having survived both types of loss, I can speak with some authority on the similarities and differences.

In both situations you are grieving not only the loss of a spouse but of the life you once had and the future you dreamed of having. My divorce left me with a strong sense of failure and defeat. As a patient once told me, the message you get as a Christian woman is you have "let the devil win." You also get the sense that others think you should be happy about the divorce. Some women even have divorce parties and celebrations! That was not my reality at all. Not wanting my children to know how sad I really was, I used my drives to and from the hospital or office to have daily meltdowns in my car.

Going through a divorce is a much more private loss than becoming a widow. No one is bringing food to your house, sending sympathy cards, or calling to see how you are doing after divorce the way they do when your husband dies. If you have young children when you divorce, not only do you lose the companionship of a husband, but you will likely have to be without the presence of your children at least every other weekend. That was the most difficult part for me. The first night my children went off to spend the weekend with their dad, I cried uncontrollably for hours!

Have you ever been in a place where you prayed the same prayer for months or even years and God's answer was a resounding, NO? What we as believers must understand beyond how much God loves us, is his sovereignty. His sovereignty trumps everything. He knows the end from the beginning. It is oh-so-easy to trust God when He answers our prayers the way we want Him to. It is the sacrifice of praise when you can still praise him in the face of tremendous loss. It is in the face of those losses that we come to understand that when we walk with God, there is always hope for the future.

"For I know the plans I have for you, declares the Lord, plans to prosper you and not to harm you, plans to give you hope and a future." Jeremiah 29:11 NIV

PRAYER

Father God, thank You for knowing the end from the beginning and for opening new doors when You close a chapter in our lives. Lord, we know that you always answer our prayers and help us to accept Your will in our lives no matter what answer You give us.

Childless by Choice

I recently saw a story on the news about the emerging trend of being childless by choice. The report cited a research study wherein 44 percent of women aged 18-40 who were not already parents said they were likely to not ever have children. According to the survey, "The reasons for not having children range from medical and financial, to concerns about the state of the world and the environment. Most participants who do not plan to have children said they simply 'just don›t want to.'" When I saw that report, I realized that childlessness is no longer the negative experience we have assumed it to be. As my own daughter once told me, "There are many different ways to live a life."

In my nearly 40 years as an ObGyn, I have encountered women who were childless due to every imaginable circumstance. Some had been pregnant and suffered multiple miscarriages. Some were married to or in relationship with someone who did not want to have children or who had undergone vasectomies. Some had abortions and inexplicably never conceived again. Some had been through many rounds of in vitro fertilization without success and given up. Some firmly believed that they had to be married to have children and were still waiting for God to send their "Boaz." Some had been forced by life-altering or life-threatening illness to have hysterectomies. And some, just like the women in that news story, had made the decision to remain childless by choice.

These days we have come to think of childless women as being in one of two groups: childless by choice and childless NOT by choice. Women in both groups face societal pressures around their childlessness that have caused them to form support groups of women who are having experiences like their own. The mere fact that support groups are needed is a reflection of the persisting stigma associated with childlessness. It is a stigma which harkens back to biblical times when a woman's very worth was tied to her ability to bear children.

There is an incredible amount of unsolicited judgment of childless women that is only now slowly beginning to change. Such attitudes must change, not only because they are wrong, but they are potentially detrimental to the mental health of childless women, regardless of WHY they are childless.

I feel so strongly about this, because several years ago a patient of mine become so depressed that a hysterectomy had left her without the ability to have children that she attempted to commit suicide! Clearly, she had been raised with the message that the inability to have children meant that she was less of a woman. Once she recovered and entered therapy, she was able to see that it is possible to live a full and productive life without motherhood.

I pray that we as Christian women will stop judging childless women and give them the love and compassion they deserve.

"Now, this is the goal: to live in harmony with one another and demonstrate affectionate love, sympathy, and kindness toward other believers. Let humility describe who you are as you dearly love one another." 1 Peter 3:8 TPT

PRAYER

Lord, please help us to show the love of Jesus to others whose life choices or circumstances may be different from the societal norms of the past. Keep us mindful that we are commanded in Your word to love one another - PERIOD.

You May be the Answer To Another's Prayer

After my divorce from the father of my children, I would tell anyone who would listen that I was never, *ever* going to marry again. I had thrown myself headlong into pro-life ministry as well as serving on the National Board of the Christian Medical and Dental Association. My relationship with God had deepened during my divorce, which had been the hardest time in my life up to that point.

I was in full-time ObGyn practice and had two very busy children to raise. I had settled into my post-divorce life and even started to embrace the freedom of the weekends that the kids spent with their dad. So, when the owner of a local restaurant approached me and asked if I was married, I replied that I was the "most not-married" woman he would ever meet. I was not only not married but absolutely not interested in ever being married again! I had to eat those words when, exactly one year later, I married that man!

So what melted my resolve to never be married again? First of all, James was a minister with a fledgling church and many of our early conversations were about the Word of God. I marveled at his knowledge and all I was learning from him. We used to joke that he "wooed me with God's word."

At the time, he had custody of his two teenage children, so we shared the highs and lows of parenting teenagers alone. He was funny. At a time in my life when my children thought I had forgotten how to smile, this man had me laughing out loud. And then there was his respecting my vow to remain celibate outside of marriage. By the time he had me entertaining the thought of getting married again, I tested him by asking him to attend premarital counseling sessions at two different churches! Surely that would be the deal breaker, but it was not!

We married on the one year anniversary of the day we met, Valentine's Day. In a bizarre coincidence, it was also the day my daddy died. Because we were both determined not to go through another divorce, we worked hard on our marriage and sought the help of a Christian counselor at the first hint of trouble.

We had family counseling when it became apparent that our two sets of children were like oil and water, not as easily blended as we would have liked. During the course of the nearly 18 years we were married, my husband suffered unspeakable tragedy, losing his two youngest children three months apart. He also lost his beloved mother, his sister and his brother. Having endured all of those losses, he was then diagnosed with stage four stomach cancer.

Fighting his cancer together, while continuing to travel and enjoy life, brought us closer than I ever knew a married couple could be.

One of the many lessons God has taught me over the course of my life is that you never know when God has a role for you to play in the life of someone else that has nothing to do with what you THINK you want or do not want. James had prayed to God for a wife at the same time I had vowed never to marry again. He loved to quote the scripture that says, "He who finds a wife finds a good thing (Proverbs 18:22)." Little did I know that, like Esther, I had been picked by God to fill that role, "for such a time as this." I now see that my growing closeness with the Lord had prepared me so that the desire of my heart changed into wanting to be the wife James had prayed for.

"Delight yourself also in the Lord, And He shall give you the desires of your heart." Psalms 37:4 NKJV

PRAYER

Father God, we thank You for teaching us to understand Your sovereign will in all situations. Let us pray as Jesus did, that not our will but Thy will be done. Lord, mold our hearts to be obedient to Your will in our lives.

Caring for the Caregiver

As we get older, the chances increase that we might be in a position to be the primary caregiver to a family member. When my late husband was in the final stages of his cancer, I took a leave of absence from my practice to become his full-time caregiver. Even as a physician, the caregiver role was one of the most challenging things I have ever done.

Many of my patients over the years have shared with me their experiences around caregiving. The one thing we could always agree on is how difficult it can be. In some cases, our loved ones angrily lash out at the very person who is trying to help them. Caregiving can take not only a physical toll on the caregiver but an emotional toll as well. The hardest thing to learn in those situations is the importance of taking care of yourself.

I have had numerous people inquire of me during the times when I was struggling as a caregiver, "Are you taking care of yourself?" I took those inquiries to heart and made conscious efforts to develop some simple strategies to keep myself healthy. Let me preface what follows by recognizing that it is the grace of God and the caring and prayers of others on my behalf that got me through the tough times. That said, I do feel that there are steps we can take when we are taking care of our loved ones that will help us to stay healthy. As the saying goes, "You cannot pour from an empty vessel!"

SELF-CARE STEPS

1. GET ENOUGH SLEEP

Sleep deprivation in and of itself is a stressor on the body. Lack of sleep and chronic stress can cause elevations in the stress hormone, cortisol. This wreaks havoc on your immune system, increasing your risk of becoming ill. It is wise to establish a good sleep routine and stick to it as much as possible during stressful times.

2. BE PHYSICALLY ACTIVE DAILY

I am sure that most of you have heard of the "runners high," which is the sense of well-being that comes from the endorphins released by running. Well, you don't have to be a runner to tap into that natural mood elevator. You can get it from any type of activity that you truly enjoy. That can be anything from a stroll in the park to dancing around your house to great music – as long as you are moving your body with purpose, it will make you feel better and will help ward off depression. There are countless workout videos available for FREE on YouTube. Often the persons requiring care sleep a lot - take advantage of those times to get in some movement.

3. DON'T EAT YOUR FEELINGS

As a lifelong emotional eater who has now adopted a healthy lifestyle, I can report that the temptation to run to comfort foods in times of stress never really goes away. Being comforted by sugary or starchy foods is embedded in our DNA. From the time we are infants, our parents and caregivers respond to every cry with a bottle or breast! It is no wonder that most of us feel a primal urge to eat in times of stress!

If you choose to try to be your healthiest self as a caregiver, you must continue to make healthy choices with your eating. Continue to choose real whole foods over starchy and processed convenience foods and drink plenty of water.

The same is also true for those who find themselves losing weight when they are caregiving because they neglect to fuel themselves properly. Eating foods that are healthy for you over the junk you may be craving takes a conscious effort. Don't let time pressures be your excuse to eat poorly. Even fast-food restaurants and grocery stores now offer salads and other healthy foods.

4. MAKE TIME FOR PRAYER

There is nothing that nourishes a struggling spirit like a strong prayer life. The comfort and security you need can often be found in daily quiet time communicating with God and meditating on His Word. Taking the time to meditate on the things you still have to be thankful for, even in the worst of times, can also help lift your spirits.

5. STAY CONNECTED TO OTHERS

The last thing you need to do as a caregiver is to isolate yourself from friends and loved ones. There is strength to be found in sharing your situation with family and close friends. Your movements may be restricted if your loved one lacks mobility, so this might be a great time to take advantage of social media, texting, Facetime, etc. Why not make it a point to text or phone a friend or distant loved one once a day?

6. BE WILLING TO ACCEPT HELP!

People do not usually offer to help you unless they mean it. They do, however, need for you to be specific about what help you need. Recognize that you cannot do it all and tap into the resources of others when you find yourself overwhelmed. A few hours of "me time" to focus just on yourself can make all the difference in the world. Taking time for a little self-care is not selfish but is necessary to your overall well-being. Look into respite care from a local nursing care facility if you do not have friends or family willing to help you take a break from time to time.

While not always easy, caregiving for a loved one is one of the most rewarding things we ever get to do. When we choose to do so, we are fulfilling a duty that comes straight from God's Holy Word.

"Be devoted to one another in love. Honor one another above yourselves." Romans 12:10 NIV

PRAYER

Lord, when we find ourselves in the position to give care to loved ones, please help us do it with willingness and humility. Please do not allow the enemy to plant seeds of resentment or bitterness. Please teach us to give care with the same love and compassion that You have given to us.

Self-Medicating with Food

I was channel surfing the other day and came across an episode of *Meet the Browns*. In this episode, Cora, a plus-sized character, wanted to fit into a particular dress, so she started power walking and restricting what she ate. After a few days, she tried on the dress and found that it was still too small and became infuriated that all of her "hard work was for nothing." She then proceeded to scarf down an entire box of candy! The portrayal touched me because it reminded me of the many times, I have turned to food to soothe an emotion. I, like millions of others who struggle with their weight, was an emotional eater.

Although we are not often conscious of it, emotional eating is very common. We eat when we are lonely or bored, we eat when we are frustrated, we eat when we are stressed, we eat when we are sad, we eat when we are angry - the list goes on and on. Emotional eating is not only about eating when we are down. We also eat when we are happy or have something to celebrate. Anytime we eat for any reason other than true physiological hunger, we are probably eating in response to an emotion.

If we are ever to overcome emotional eating, we must seek to understand why we have this love affair with food. It is a love affair with a lover who *does not love us back* and who also abuses our bodies. There is a reason why certain foods are referred to as comfort foods. Foods high in fat, sugar, and/or salt activate the brain's reward system. Processed food manufacturers know this and intentionally produce products that reach the magical combination of sugar, fat, and salt known as the "bliss point." We get an increased sense of well-being when we eat certain foods. Chocolate, for example, has a strong effect on mood by increasing pleasant feelings and reducing tension. If the food makes us feel better, then the next time we have an intense emotion we are more likely to turn to food again.

The reality, of course, is that the fix is only temporary, and the guilt and weight gain gives us more problems to stress over, which leads to more overeating. When we eat when we are sad, lonely, tired, or bored, we are self-medicating with food. The cliche of the heartbroken girl eating ice cream straight out of a container after she has been dumped by her boyfriend is depicted over and over on TV and in the movies. It turns out that sugary foods like ice cream increase the dopamine levels in our brains and act as an antidepressant. Is there any wonder why so many of us are addicted to processed junk foods?

With the medical complications of obesity on the rise, we need to find ways to decrease emotional eating in our efforts to become our healthiest selves. One of the best ways to overcome emotional eating is to get reacquainted with true physiological hunger as the primary reason why we should eat. Observe the average two-year-old. Most of them will let you know when they are hungry, eat a very small amount, and then tell you they are full. We get disconnected from that God-given mechanism of hunger and fullness when our well-meaning parents demand that we "clean our plates" and through a lifetime of recreational eating of highly processed foods. Each time we have the urge to eat, we need to pause and ask ourselves if we are truly "stomach growling" hungry or do we just want to eat for some other reason. If we determine that we are not physically hungry, we need to find other ways to satisfy the urge to use food to handle our emotions.

In times like this, we need a game plan for doing something other than eating to make ourselves feel better. The possibilities of other activities that will give us that mood elevation we seek include taking a brisk walk or run, going for a bike ride, taking a Yoga or Pilates class, reading a book, listening to music, prayer or meditation - the possibilities are endless! Vow to no longer be the person who eats their feelings but one who manages her feelings in healthier ways.

"I have the right to do anything, you say—but not everything is beneficial. I have the right to do anything—but I will not be mastered by anything."
1 Corinthians 6:12 NIV

PRAYER

Lord, we ask for Your forgiveness when we turn to anyone or anything other than You to deal with our emotions. You blessed us with food to use as fuel for our bodies, not to heal our emotions.

My Diabetes Legacy

Although I saw very little of my father growing up, one day when I was with him stands out. My dad's mother was in the hospital, and he took me with him to visit her. What I did not know was that my paternal grandmother had suffered gangrene in both her legs from her out-of-control diabetes. As a result, she had to have a double above-the-knee amputation! I can still remember vividly seeing her in the hospital bed with nearly half of her body missing. I had never seen or heard of such a thing, and it horrified me!

I knew that my father had diabetes as well because I had watched him give himself insulin. He had the notion that if he took insulin every day, he could eat and drink whatever he wanted. Never was I told that sugar was the poison that took my grandmother's legs, let alone that the same thing could happen to me!

I am not sure when my love affair with food began, but as a child, I loved two things, books and food. I come from a long line of great soul food cooks. I can remember sitting at my grandmother's kitchen table eating fried chicken, rice, gravy, and biscuits, and having to unfasten my skirt so I could eat more. There was a little store up the street that sold "two for a penny" cookies. I could get 10 cookies for a nickel and eat them all before I got home. By the time I was 14, I tipped the scales at 185 lbs. on my small 5' 5" frame.

It was as I was about to enter high school that I discovered dieting. I found that by skipping breakfast and having a salad and diet soda for lunch, I could still eat a "normal dinner." Throughout high school, college, med school, residency, and for most of my adult life, I was the queen of the yo-yo dieters. My motivation was the fear of becoming a size 20 again! You name the diet; I have tried it. I also had a large collection of exercise videos that I used consistently, thinking they would help me keep the weight off. The problem was that I still loved to eat and always drifted back to the foods I loved as a child. I have lost and regained the same 20 pounds countless times.

It was not until I was well into my 50s with persisting hypertension, and my growing knowledge of how dangerous that could be, that I joined a local fitness group for accountability to get healthy. We were required to do some 5K races each year and I started to enjoy them.

After doing several of those, I took on the challenge of the half marathon distance and started doing them regularly. Ultimately and to my amazement I ended up doing a half marathon in every state! The fat kid had morphed into a distance runner! Who would have thought such a thing was possible?

Somewhere in the middle of doing all those half marathons, I found myself not only still hypertensive but now also a pre-diabetic! My genetics and my love affair with food had caught up with me! Running did not save me from my genes - you simply cannot outrun a bad diet. Over the last few years, I have taken the time to educate myself on the PERMANENT lifestyle changes I needed to successfully reverse my own health issues. I have used what I have learned as the basis for my healthy living blog: ymoore4health. com. It has become my passion to teach others what I have learned from the mistakes I made with my own health. I invite you to visit the blog if you too are ready to make the permanent lifestyle changes you need to become your healthiest self.

"Dear friend, I hope all is well with you and that you are as healthy in body as you are strong in spirit." 3 John 1:2 NLT

PRAYER

Lord, thank you for the bodies You have given us to be temples for the Holy Spirit. Please give us the wisdom to make lifestyle choices that will contribute to good health. It is when we are at our healthiest that we can be fit to do the assignments You have for us in Kingdom building.

Confession of a Mindless Eater

Growing up, I was a "latchkey kid." From the age of 10 through high school, I was home alone between 4 pm and 11 pm every day. I was not allowed to have company, so my friends were the television and food. I ate dinner alone in front of the TV every weekday! Studies have shown that eating in front of the TV, computer, or while scrolling on our phones impairs our ability to recognize when we are full and leads to chronic overeating. Even if you are eating healthy foods, the tendency is still to overeat! No wonder I became an obese teenager!

Recently, I have been studying the concept of mindfulness as it applies to many areas of our lives. To be mindful is to be fully present and engaged in the moment without dwelling on the past or the future. Even the Bible instructs us, "not to worry about tomorrow for it will take care of itself (Matthew 6:34)." Mindfulness is also about focus and concentration without distractions.

The opposite of mindfulness is mindlessness. We all have moments of mindlessness. Have you ever been reading a book or an article and had to go back and reread a section because you didn't know what you just read? Your eyes may have been scanning the page, but your mind was somewhere else. Something similar happens when we eat while doing other things. When we don't give our eating our full attention at the moment, we are eating mindlessly and likely to eat beyond what we truly need to eat to stay healthy.

Here are just a few examples of mindless eating:

- Eating anytime you are not physically hungry or continuing to eat beyond fullness
- Standing at the refrigerator or pantry nibbling on whatever is there
- Eating directly from a large container of food
- Eating while watching TV, scrolling social media, reading, or working – this can lead to overeating

- Eating popcorn at the movies or a hotdog at a sporting event out of habit when you have just had a full meal. I call this recreational eating.
- Eating because someone left treats in the break room at work.
- Eating because you are sad, angry, lonely, frustrated, or tired or because you are happy or celebrating, also known as emotional eating.

The good news is that mindless eating is a learned behavior, which means it can be unlearned. Lifestyle changes that lead to better health are often a matter of breaking bad habits and developing new, more beneficial habits. Learning to eat mindfully takes effort but it can be done.

TIPS TO HELP YOU GET STARTED

Before you sit down to eat, ask yourself if you are truly physically hungry or if you are eating for some other reason. Once you identify that you are just bored, for example, find another way to deal with that boredom. Remember that physical hunger is the

God-given mechanism to let us know when to eat. Physical hunger is like that light that comes on in your car when your fuel is low. We just must learn to listen to it.

Do not eat a meal or a snack unless you are sitting down with a plate or bowl instead of eating from a container.

Avoid eating in your car or standing up.

Give your food your full attention by eating without multitasking with the TV, a book, a computer, or a phone. If you must eat alone, use mealtime as a quiet time for reflection and gratitude. Take the time to appreciate the taste, aroma, and texture of your food. If you do not like eating in silence, try playing some low-volume soft jazz or instrumental gospel music in the background. It can make mealtime a very relaxing experience and a great way to de-stress.

Eat slowly and stop when you are comfortably full. It takes a full 20 minutes for your brain to realize your stomach is full. Pause between bites and sip water to slow you down. If you eat too fast you are more likely to overeat.

I challenge all of us to learn to eat without distraction as a pathway to better health.

"Set your gaze on the path before you. With fixed purpose, looking straight ahead, ignore life's distractions." Proverbs 4:25 TPT

PRAYER

Lord, please remind us of how to use our God-given cues of hunger and fullness to help us develop a healthy relationship with food. Help us to be good stewards of these bodies You have given us to live in with behaviors that help us to avoid overeating because it can be a gateway to obesity and chronic disease.

Love the Foods that Love You Back

When it comes to using food to help you lose weight and/or just be healthier, there can be a lot of confusion about what constitutes the healthiest eating plan. If we are trying to eat in a way that will promote our best health, we should not get the idea that one eating plan fits all.

Take me, for example. I am a 70-year-old, pre-diabetic with a history of hypertension and childhood obesity. A LCHF (low carb healthy fat) lifestyle, along with regular exercise, is the approach that has made me healthier now than I was 20 years ago. Others whose medical profile or personal preferences are different might not find this approach either desirable or sustainable long-term.

That said, I believe some universal concepts hold true no matter what WOE (way of eating) we choose.

One of those concepts is **you must learn to love the foods that love you back!** Often, when I try to advise patients on healthy eating, they tell me that they cannot sustain a long-term healthy eating plan because they "love" ice cream (chips or cookies or cornbread, etc.). My response to anyone who has struggled with their weight for this reason is typically, "What has ice cream ever done for you?"

Having an unshakeable love for foods that are unhealthy for you is like being in a relationship with someone who is physically abusing you. The victim keeps letting the abuser back into their life expecting it to be different this time, but it rarely is! We can't keep returning to eating sugary foods, french fries, and other junk foods every day and expecting them to make us healthy this time around. That is part of the reason why so many people who lose a significant amount of weight gain it back within two years!

If you want something you've never had, you must do something you've never done. Resolve that this time will be different! I understand the passion we have for food because I LOVE to eat. That love led me to take up running in my late fifties with the notion that I would "run so I could eat whatever I wanted." That turned out to be a big, fat lie! Contrary to popular belief, you cannot "outrun" a bad diet.

We need to acknowledge that we eat as much for enjoyment as we do for fuel. We just must train ourselves to love the foods that not only taste good but also reward us with positive changes in our health. When you commit to eating in a way that promotes good health, why not take the focus off the foods you should no longer eat and instead focus on learning to love those foods that you know are good for you? The disease-causing foods like sugar and sugary drinks, processed carbs (junk food) and deep-fried foods have no place in your pursuit of good health.

Regardless of which healthy eating plan you choose long-term, you will be told to reduce or eliminate your intake of these foods. Instead of mourning the loss of the "bad" foods you shouldn't eat, look at them as the poisons they are and get excited about all the wonderful things you get to enjoy eating and still be healthy. As Hippocrates so famously said, "Food is medicine." Every bite you eat is either promoting good health or disease. You can take control of your health by making this simple shift in your mindset! LEARN TO LOVE THE FOODS THAT LOVE YOU BACK!!!

"Why spend your money on food that does not give you strength? Why pay for food that does you no good? Listen to me, and you will eat what is good. You will enjoy the finest food." Isaiah 55:2 NLT

PRAYER

Lord, we ask you to deliver us from any addictions we might have to unhealthy foods. We ask the Holy Spirit to lead us away from foods that are not good for our health and well-being. Help us learn to love the foods and behaviors that will keep our temples free from disease.

Becoming a Widow
Hope After Loss

In 2016 my late husband, James, was a vibrant, active 72-year-old guy who still worked part-time and was an avid golfer as well as an associate pastor at our church. He had to have cataract surgery and needed a driver, so I took off work to bring him. It wasn't until they weighed him, and he had lost 30lbs without even trying that I realized that something was wrong. He had no other symptoms except for a single episode of what we thought was food poisoning the week before.

I insisted that he go to his PCP who sent him to a GI doctor who initially said it was ulcers, yet he took several biopsies. Because I had access to his chart as one of his "referring" physicians, I pulled up the pathology report before the doctor had a chance to call us and saw "extensive adenocarcinoma of the stomach" in every biopsy. I prayed that I was in a nightmare and that I would wake up relieved.

Within a few weeks, we found out that the cancer was stage 4 - treatable but not curable with a 5% cure rate, and an average survival of 18 months. But God . . .

From the very beginning, we enlisted every prayer warrior we knew to pray for and with us. We committed to fight this cancer together but also to continue to live our lives. By then I was chasing a goal of completing a half marathon in every state and he traveled with me between treatments and played golf wherever I ran. People marveled at how active he was able to be while fighting cancer.

We gave testimony to the goodness of God every chance we got. God rewarded our faith with three and a half years of what He intended marriage to be. I had often said after my divorce from my children's father that I would never marry again. Once again, God's plan trumped my own. I truly believe that when James prayed for a wife, God answered him with me, "For such a time as this."

My experience with becoming a widow started before my husband passed away, with the anticipatory grief of having a spouse with terminal cancer. When the cancer returned after three years in remission, it came back in the cruelest of ways. I became not only his cheerleader but his primary caregiver, taking a leave of absence from work to care for him.

Women whose husbands die suddenly must deal with the shock of sudden loss, but they are spared the "long goodbye" of watching the progressive deterioration of someone they love. At the very end, I had crawled into bed with him and had my head on his chest listening to his final heartbeats. It was a moment I will never forget, excruciatingly painful and beautiful at the same time.

In a godly marriage, the phrase "the two shall become as one" means that a part of you dies along with your spouse. Everyone grieves differently and even the same person grieves differently for each person they lose. There is no playbook, no timetable, and no right or wrong way to grieve. We do ourselves a disservice when we expect to be "over" our grief at a certain time.

Fortunately, for us as believers, we do not have to grieve as those who have no hope. God left us instructions in 1st Thessalonians that we are to encourage one another with the knowledge that death is not the end of the story:

"For since we believe that Jesus died and was raised to life again, we also believe that when Jesus returns, God will bring back with him the believers who have died. Then, together with them, we who are still alive and remain on the earth will be caught up in the clouds to meet the Lord in the air. Then we will be with the Lord forever." 1 Thessalonians 4:14, 17 NLT

PRAYER

Father God, we thank You for the gift of salvation that has conquered death. As we experience sadness when a loved one dies, remind us that they are not really lost because we know that to be absent from the body is to be present with the Lord. Please give us the comfort that only You can give.

Mama Bear
Hope for Orphaned Adults

If you look up the term "godmother" in the dictionary you will see something about the person that one's parents agree should care for a child if something happens to them. There is often a formal service like a baptism where she is introduced to the world as that person.

But what if a child outlives both her parents and godparents and finds herself in need of mothering? That is exactly what happened in the case of my "goddaughter." It is unusual for two adult women nearly 20 years apart in age to develop a close friendship in midlife. We started as doctor and patient, then friends, and found in the course of conversations that we liked the same movies, television shows, and music and that we both deeply loved the Lord.

I had recently lost my mother, my husband, and a very dear friend in rapid succession while she still very much missed her late mother to whom she was very close. In a manner uncharacteristic for both of us, we started sharing what we called "Vegas" conversations where we told each other things about ourselves that very few other people knew. Ours was an unlikely friendship between a widow and an orphan - one that I am now convinced was ordained by God.

Our bond became solidified once we found out that a medical condition she suffered from for years had become life-threatening and could only be treated with a lung transplant. She already had several good girlfriends closer to her age, as well as siblings who were amazing in their love and support, but God knew she needed to have that "mama" void filled for what she was about to face.

As I look back now, it is remarkable how God had her pick me to fill that role. When things started to get particularly tough, she turned to me for advice, a listening ear, or an honest assessment of when she was acting like a "brat" (her term, not mine). I became so fiercely protective of her that she dubbed me her "Mama Bear." The journey is arduous just to simply get listed for a lung transplant, but it pales in comparison to the surgery itself and the weeks and weeks of recovery.

When God gives you an assignment, you know for sure that it came from Him when you feel it in your spirit in a way that cannot be shaken. Satan tried to get me to back away from yet another person with a life-threatening illness, but the Holy Spirit just would not let me do it.

Instead, I came to love and fight for my "bonus daughter" in ways that surprised even me. When she expressed concern that I had already been through enough, I asked her who could better walk alongside her than someone who had been there before. That is how God works and He might even let you think it was your idea. When you feel God's calling on your life, you might try to run but you cannot hide. Just take the assignment, do it to the best of your ability and He will bless you for it!

They need to add a second definition to "Godmother" to describe what happens when God Himself provides an orphaned adult with a "bonus" mom. What an honor it has been to be chosen by Him to fill that role during this season of my life.

"True spirituality that is pure in the eyes of our
Father God is to make a difference in the lives of the
orphans, and widows in their troubles, and to refuse
to be corrupted by the world's values."
James 1:27 TPT

PRAYER

*Lord, we thank You for the divine assignments You
place on our lives. Help us to recognize them when they
are presented and to use them for Your glory and not
our own. Lord, we thank You for giving us the means
and opportunity to show Your love to others.*

Dementia
Losing the Same Person Twice

My grandmother raised me. For most of that upbringing, it was just the two of us in our house. I often wonder what would have become of me had she not been willing to parent me. My Aunt Merle, my mother's youngest sister, had been 15 years old when I was born, and I adored her. I was HER baby as a toddler, following her around like a little puppy. I was heartbroken when she got married to a guy who was in the Army and left us to travel with him. For as long as I can remember, these two women were the most important people in my life. It was not until I had finished medical school and moved back to Memphis that my grandmother, by then in her eighties, started to have trouble with her memory.

It was subtle at first, as she began leaving out key ingredients when cooking or forgetting to pay bills.

Ultimately, she began forgetting that she had put something in the oven and fell victim to neighbors who took her shopping and spent her money on themselves. My aunt decided that she needed to move MaDear to D.C. so she could take care of her. I visited as often as I could while in full-time practice and raising a family.

On one visit, I found her in her room with a clock radio in her lap trying to call my aunt on the "phone." I soon learned that her dementia was getting worse. On one of our last visits, she thought I was one of her childhood friends. Although I was so sad that she no longer knew me, I played along as she reminisced with the friend, she thought I was. I knew then that this dear lady who sacrificed so much for me was now gone, replaced by someone who no longer even recognized her "Pookie."

At this writing, my adored aunt also has dementia. She has always been the person I would go to when I needed encouragement, a shoulder to cry on, or a listening ear. We had so many inside jokes between us, and we both loved music of all kinds. That person is no longer there and has been replaced by someone who repeats the same questions every few seconds and has delusions that she still drives and goes to work. Often when I visit, she thinks I am my late mother and asks me about people they knew in childhood. This sweet soul took care of both my grandmother and my mother in the last years of their lives and will forever be my hero.

Dementia is the cruelest disease in that it takes the sufferer not once but twice. If you have watched a loved one slowly disappear, you likely understand that the progressive grief you feel is just as real as the grief you feel when a loved one dies. The sad emotions I now feel after every conversation with my aunt reflects that grief. In both situations, I have marveled at how well long-term memory is preserved in those with dementia. The highlight of every visit with both of them has been playing and singing along with Gospel songs. During those times God has allowed praise and worship to make me feel as if I still had a part of them with me.

Even though I, like you, may not understand why my loved ones developed dementia, I trust in the God who made us all, and I am grateful He has kept His praises and His word alive in their hearts!

"My heart is steadfast, O God, my heart is steadfast; I will sing and give praise." Psalms 57:7 NKJV

PRAYER

Dear Lord, as we mourn the loss of those in our lives who suffer from dementia, please give us the patience to meet them where they are at any given moment. Help us to see that the anger and rage that often come with this illness is not coming from the loved one but from this cruel disease. Please give us Your strength and heal our broken hearts.

Being a Titus 2 Woman

When I first started my career in private practice 40 years ago, I was a member of an all-female ObGyn group, and we were enough of a rarity that most of our older male colleagues referred to us as "the girls." We saw it as sexist and disrespectful and did not like it one bit. As time went on, other all-female groups emerged and many more women entered our field, so we eventually lost that moniker. (I realized recently that it has been quite some time since anyone has called me "girl.")

It seems to me that at 70 I have very quickly made the transition from a young, inexperienced doctor to a seasoned practitioner who is now taking care of young women I delivered over thirty years ago. I am now seeing the moms through menopause and their daughters through young adulthood. If you stay in a profession long enough, you will eventually be servicing two and, in some cases, three generations of people. Just ask any schoolteacher who finds herself teaching the children of the children she taught many years ago. As a gynecologist, I have always looked at it as a supreme compliment when one of my patients brings her daughter to me because I was the person who delivered her. What a blessing!

As I am now taking care of not only baby boomers but Millennials and GenXers, I have tried to keep up with the times so that I can speak their language and relate to the angst of young women in their 20s and 30s. I maintain a pretty robust social media presence for just that reason. As a Christian physician, I often must walk a tightrope between my strong sense of right and wrong based on biblical principles and my desire to meet young women where they are.

Many times, we have to agree to disagree on topics like premarital sex or actively pursuing pregnancy before marriage. At that point, I see my role as an educator as much as a doctor and try to teach them how their bodies work and what they need to do to protect the health of their reproductive organs and their future fertility.

I feel as if that little six-year-old inside me who wanted nothing more than to be a teacher has come full circle as I use pelvic models and other visual aids to help them understand what is sometimes the mystery of a woman's body.

That is what the older woman referred to in Titus 2 is charged to do - teach the younger women by example "what is right and good." That charge is given to all women of a certain age.

If you have been privileged to live a long life, as I have, consider passing along some of what you have learned along the way to the younger women in your sphere of influence. Consider it your duty to do so.

"Older women similarly are to be reverent in their behavior, not malicious gossips nor addicted to much wine, teaching what is right and good."
Titus 2:3 AMP

PRAYER

Lord, scripture is very clear about what is expected of older women in the body of Christ. Help us to follow those instructions by living in a godly manner before the younger women in our lives. Please give us opportunities to teach them what is "right and good."

Widowing Well
Using Grief for Good

I recently had a conversation with a fellow widow who was disturbed that some of her late husband's coworkers had passed away and no one bothered to tell her. I shared with her that she was not alone in feeling disconnected from people she had known for years when her husband was alive. I shared with her that over the years I have experienced a "falling away" of the people who were a part of my husband's inner circle but not necessarily a part of mine. The term *the two shall become as one* means that once your spouse is gone, some people act as if you are gone as well. We are all guilty of overestimating our significance in the lives of others. That is why it is important to carve out a new life for yourself amid your grief so you can become a whole person again.

A dear friend who spoke at my husband's memorial service talked about the legacy that James left to us by the way he handled his diagnosis of stage 4 cancer. Rather than curl up in a ball and have a pity party, he took it in stride and did not let it stop him from living life to the fullest. He would get treatments and two days later we would be off on one of our many golf/run mini vacations. She said that he gave us the blueprint for what it means to "suffer well." I watched him do this not only during his cancer treatment but also during the loss of his mother as well as his two youngest children. Of course, he grieved, but he continued to play his beloved golf, study, and teach the Word of God, and enjoy his life. So, when I heard the phrase "suffer well," I asked God to give me the strength to "widow well."

On the first anniversary of his death, I wrote these words to my late husband: "…You taught me by example how to keep living life to the fullest regardless of what adversity comes our way. You taught me to trust God no matter what! Giving up is not an option! I am so grateful for the life lessons I learned just being your wife. You were my forever hero, my travel buddy, my date night partner, my sports tutor, my lover, and my very best friend. I miss your bear hugs, your corny jokes, and your laugh -

you had the best laugh ever! I miss you more than I have words to express. I praise God for keeping me even in my lowest moments. Rest on, my sweet hubby, my love for you will never die."

What a legacy he left to all of us who loved him! I pray to continue to "widow well," by living my remaining years to the fullest, following the blueprint he left for me. Over the time since I wrote that, God has helped me to understand what it means to "widow well."

You widow well when you reach out to others in their time of loss and offer them your time and your prayers for the same peace and comfort you have received. You widow well by continuing to do those things that bring you joy, even if you must do them alone, fully realizing that you are never really alone because Jesus is always with you. You widow well when you draw close to God by digging deeper into His word and living your life accordingly. You widow well when you stay engaged with people in whatever way God leads you. There is no better way to honor the legacy of a loved one than by living abundantly in the way they would have wanted you to live!

"He comforts us in all our troubles so that we can comfort others. When they are troubled, we will be able to give them the same comfort God has given us." 2 Corinthians 1:4 NLT

PRAYER

Dear Lord, as widows we have become members of the club no one wants to be a part of – the widows club. Thank You for Your comfort and compassion as You heal our broken hearts. Thank You for allowing me to inspire others that a widow's life can be a full life because of You. I pray that every widow will find the strength to "widow well."

Textspirations
Using Technology to Spread Hope

A few years ago, I decided to use my social media accounts to share at least one of the several devotionals I read during my morning quiet time. There is so much negativity on social media, that I wanted to bring balance to my news feed by posting insights from the Word of God daily.

What I have seen consistently over the years is that those posts get seen by far fewer people than the rest of my posts. I am convinced that the algorithms are set up that way. It would be just like the enemy to undermine efforts to spread the Word of God! It is my prayer that the posts are shared by those who do see them, so they are seen by the persons who need them.

More recently, I was deeply touched by a patient I have taken care of for over 30 years who got a diagnosis of breast cancer. The Lord laid it in my heart to walk the journey with her by sending a daily inspirational text message that included a Bible passage and/or a prayer along with the link to a gospel song. Anyone who knows me knows that I LOVE gospel music. During the final stages of my late husband's illness, and to this day, my therapy has been long walks and road trips taken while listening to gospel music. So many of those songs have lyrics that come straight from the Word of God, and I know from experience that they have the power to heal!

What started with a single patient has widened into a ministry that I call "morning textpirations." There are now well over 100 people who get the texts daily with the intent that they will be shared with other people who may need a little encouragement. It has been very gratifying to hear that people I have never met are now receiving the Word of God and gospel music to start their days. What a blessing it has been in my life to be used by God to spread His love to others!

"Listen to my voice in the morning, Lord. Each morning, I bring my requests to you and wait expectantly." Psalms 5:3 NLT

PRAYER

Lord, I thank You that although You are the same yesterday, today, and tomorrow, You continue to give us new ways to reach one another with love and encouragement. The enemy may have intended for social media to be his tool to reach others for his purposes, but You continue to inspire us with ways to use it for Your glory.

Successful Aging
Hope for the Golden Years

"You never know when the sand is
going to run out of the hourglass."
-Author Unknown

Ultimately, we all die. We have no control over
this. What we do have is at least some control over
the quality of that life. As Christians, we believe
that Jesus came so that we might have an abundant
life. To me, that means that we can have lives full
of joy and strength for spirit, soul, and body even
as we get older.

Successful aging, according to neuroscientist,
David Levitan, involves decreasing the probability of
disease and disease-related disability, intact cognitive
functioning, and active engagement with life. The

goal should be to be able to do whatever you want to do for as long as you can.

As I am coming to the end of my seventh decade of life, experience has taught me a few "must-do" behaviors that are helping me to truly enjoy my golden years.

1. YOU MUST EAT AS IF YOUR LIFE DEPENDED ON IT.

Whatever way of eating gets you to your healthiest self must be maintained over the long haul. Regardless of which type of eating that is, it must minimize sugars, simple starches, and processed foods. Healthy eating as you grow older means generous amounts of protein to combat muscle loss and should focus on simple, single-ingredient, whole foods.

2. YOU SIMPLY MUST KEEP MOVING!

Movement, like food, is medicine. Aim for 30 minutes of simple, safe exercise you enjoy most days of the week. It does not have to be structured but it does need to be consistent. In addition to weight-bearing exercises like walking, be sure to do some resistance training, as well as exercises that improve flexibility and balance. There are hundreds of FREE videos on YouTube that demonstrate all of these.

3. YOU MUST GET ADEQUATE SLEEP.

Most people think that our need for sleep declines with age when in actuality it becomes MORE important as we age. During sleep, our bodies repair themselves, and our batteries get recharged. The time-honored advice of trying to sleep at least eight hours a night becomes crucial as we get older.

4. YOU MUST LEARN TO RELAX AND TO REST PERIODICALLY.

The concept of rest is so important that God included it in the 10 commandments. Rest and relaxation are crucial to our ability to handle the stresses of everyday living. Daily quiet time in prayer and worship has become a non-negotiable part of my life that I highly recommend.

5. YOU MUST GET OUTSIDE IN NATURE AS OFTEN AS YOU CAN, ESPECIALLY ON SUNNY DAYS.

The sense of well-being that comes from getting fresh air and sunshine comes from the release of serotonin, the feel-good hormone. The sun also boosts vitamin D which is important to bone health. The benefit of as little as a 15-minute walk outside in nature is priceless.

6. YOU MUST KEEP YOUR MIND ENGAGED BY CONTINUING TO LEARN NEW THINGS, VISITING NEW PLACES, MEETING NEW PEOPLE, AND STAYING CONNECTED WITH OTHERS.

Take an online class. Join a book club. Try a new form of exercise, make some new recipes, learn a new language, how to play an instrument, memorize scripture, or get a new hobby. You may choose to stay engaged by delaying retirement by working part-time and/or doing some volunteer work. The possibilities are endless.

7. YOU MUST HAVE FUN!!!

"Now that I am old and gray, do not abandon me, O God. Let me proclaim your power to this new generation, your mighty miracles to all who come after me." Psalms 71:18 NLT

PRAYER

Lord, we realize that longevity is a privilege that some are not given. For those of us who are blessed to have it, guide us into making the best of our "golden years." As we get older, please bless us with the wisdom to take care of ourselves so that we can continue to live the abundant life until You call us home.

Traveling Solo But Never Alone

Earlier this year, I met a lovely 88-year-old woman who, having raised a family and beat lung cancer, finds herself living alone. I did not know that she lived alone when I met her, but when the topic came up in conversation she said, "I may be the only person who lives in my house, but I am never alone!" I knew exactly what she meant, and she and I made an instant connection because we each have a relationship with Jesus that guarantees that we are never alone.

One of my favorite things to do is to take road trips and explore cities I have never visited (I am a self-proclaimed museum geek). When I am chastised for traveling alone, I always reply that "everywhere I go I take my Jesus with me."

Perhaps because I was raised as an only child by a grandmother who worked the second shift, I have always been comfortable being alone. As a child, television, books, and food were my best friends during the many hours I spent alone. My love for food ultimately led to childhood obesity which further isolated me because I was often bullied and ridiculed about my weight. I was able to find solace in becoming the best student I could be. I might not have been able to conquer the high jump in gym class, but I could get good grades! Spending so much time alone just felt normal to me because I never had it any other way.

Both as a wife and as a mother, my need for alone time was an inner struggle that I never talked about but was always there. My adult children still joke about how I would call to say I was on my way home from the office that was 10 minutes away, but I wouldn't get home for another hour. Sometimes I would pull into the garage and just sit in my car for several minutes to "decompress" after a day of listening to other people's problems.

I have had a few seasons of singleness in my life, both before and between my marriages but my current season of widowhood is the first time since my 20s that I am not either raising children and/

or being a wife. The irony is that now that I have all the alone time I secretly craved, I feel less alone than I ever have because of the deeply personal relationship I have with Jesus! He is with me every second of every minute of every day. My dialogue with Him is ongoing throughout my day. I depend on Him to give me the wise counsel that I pass along to my patients and others in my life. My favorite times are when I say something to someone that I KNOW came directly from the Holy Spirit and not from my head!

Miss Sylvia at 88 and I at 70 have learned the secret of being content as single people. It is a lesson that I wish I had known in my previous seasons of singleness, but one I am oh-so-grateful to know now. If you are reading this and lamenting your singleness, I can testify to you that there is joy and peace to be found in getting to know Jesus personally. Take advantage of your season of singleness to drown yourself in the Word of God. Take a Bible study class, join an intercessory prayer group, and learn how to listen to the Holy Spirit as He leads and guides you. That way, even if your single days come to an end, you will be bringing a better, more complete you to your next season!

"I am not saying this because I am in need, for I have learned to be content whatever the circumstances." Philippians 4:11 NIV

PRAYER

Lord, I thank You for the gift of contentment. I pray that anyone who finds themselves in a season of singleness will recognize it as an opportunity to wallow in Your Word and become closer to You.

Letter to My Younger Self

Dear Yvonne,

I saw you at Bellevue Junior High a couple of times this week. The first time, I saw one of your friends walk up to you and hug you while calling you "Charmin," because you are so squeezably soft. You laughed it off, but I could tell it hurt your feelings. The second time I saw you bluff your way out of a confrontation with the tough girl in your class by telling her that all you had to do was sit on her to shut her up, so she didn't want to mess with you. I saw you repeatedly use self-deprecating humor to mask your unhappiness. You may be one of the smartest girls in the class, but you only see yourself as the fat girl who had to special order gym clothes because they did not come in your size. I want you to know that in the future you will lose weight and no longer be defined by your size. Believe it or not, there will be a time in your life when you will come to love exercise and healthy eating and will help others to become their healthiest selves.

You will be chosen to work on the junior high school newspaper, and you will fall in love with writing. You will decide to become a writer/journalist. That ambition will have to wait because you will not be chosen for the high school newspaper staff. You will be very disappointed, but God has a different plan for your life.

You will be accepted at Washington University in St. Louis, where you will go with the intent to become a physical therapist. You will forever be an avid sports fan, especially of your beloved St. Louis Cardinals. You will get to go see them play in the World Series, not once but twice!

Having been a good little church girl your entire life, you will use your freedom in college to try to become a bad girl. You will do a lot of things you will live to regret. You will experience a lot of guilt during those times, but you will also have a lot of fun.

God's plan for your life will take you to medical school instead of physical therapy school and into a career as an OB-GYN. You will deliver hundreds of babies and perform hundreds of operations over a career that will span over 40 years.

I know you think you don't want kids, but you will get married after residency and later give birth to a wonderful daughter and son and you will LOVE being a mom. Because of their father's job, you will travel to many places including England, France, and the Netherlands. Your marriage will end after 15 years, and you will be devastated - but you will survive. You, like many others in a crisis, will find your way back to the close relationship with God that you had abandoned in college. It will be the strength you draw from God that will sustain you during your season as a divorced single parent.

Even though you will be determined to never get married again, you will. Your last marriage will be to a restaurant owner who also happens to be a minister. You will bond over loving God, studying scripture, and a mutual love for sports and travel. You will find a wonderful church to serve in. The people there will become like family to you. You will see each other through unspeakable tragedies and losses, which will only make you closer. You will attend multiple sporting events, including those two World Series, an NBA Finals game, and a Super Bowl.

You will be supportive of his golf addiction, and he will travel with you to most of your races as you chase the goal of completing a half marathon in every state. No, seriously, I know it is hard for your little chubby self to believe it, but you really will accomplish this! But you won't even get started down that path until well into your 50s. You will prove to many that it is never too late.

Even though your parents chose to let MaDear raise you, you will make your peace and grow to love them despite the resentment you feel right now. You will be able to help all three of them navigate the illnesses they experience at the end of their lives and will be blessed by doing so. Like all the women in your family, you will ultimately become a widow, but not before experiencing the joy of a godly marriage.

Amid your grief, you will make the most of your season of widowhood by continuing to practice medicine part-time into your seventies and you will continue to do races, travel, attend concerts and sporting events, and serve the Lord by serving others. You are even going to finally become the writer you always dreamed of being, first as a blogger and then as a published author!

I am sure that what I am telling you seems impossible to you. Even if you don't believe me, the one thing that I want you to know is that your life will prove that "with God all things are possible."

About the Author

YVONNE MORE

Yvonne Frank Moore, MD, MA, FACOG is a native Memphian and a board-certified OB/GYN who has been in private practice since 1984. She holds BA in biology and psychology from Washington University in St. Louis and her medical degree was earned at St. Louis University. Feeling the need to incorporate Christian counseling into her practice, in 2007 she earned a master's degree in human relations from Liberty University. She has served or is currently serving on numerous boards and hospital committees over the years.

She is the widow of the late Rev. James Lee Moore, Jr. and the mother to two adult children, Kyra and Justin Sims. She is an active member of True Light Baptist Church where she part of the social media team, A Minute for Your Health, and the book club. She is also the volunteer wellness coach for Dreamgirls Healthier You, a virtual support group of ladies from all over the country who simply want to become their healthiest selves.

Dr. Moore is an avid sports fan and an enthusiastic interval runner. She is a perennial St. Jude Hero, running to raise funds for St. Jude Children's Research Hospital. In 2021 she completed the challenge of finishing at least one, half marathon in each of the 50 states, DC, and Puerto Rico. She is now pursuing the goal of completing 100 half marathons having now done 85 of them at this writing.

Since retiring from delivering babies, her medical practice focuses on gynecology and helping her patients live healthier lives through positive lifestyle and behavioral changes. It truly has become a passion for her! She writes a blog for her patients about various topics on healthy living particularly as we age. The blog address is ymoore4health.com.

Sharing scriptures and prayers with patients allows to her to bring the love of Jesus to her interactions with patients. Dr. Moore has been quoted as saying that her close personal relationship with God has transformed her from "a doctor who happens to be a Christian into a Christian who just happens to be a doctor."

Proceeds from the sale of this book will be donated to Dr. Moore's annual fundraising efforts for St. Jude's Children's Research Hospital.